RELEARNING THE ALPHABET

Books by Denise Levertov

Poetry

The Double Image

Here and Now

Overland to the Islands

With Eyes at the Back of Our Heads

The Jacob's Ladder

O Taste and See

The Sorrow Dance

Relearning the Alphabet

Translations

Guillevic/Selected Poems

Denise Levertov

Relearning the Alphabet

A New Directions Book

Acknowledgments

Some of these poems first appeared in the following magazines, to whose editors grateful acknowledgment is made by the author and publisher: *Apple, Chelsea, "Today's Poets" (Chicago Tribune), Dance Perspectives, Descant, El Corno Emplumado, Fubbalo, Journal for the Protection of All Beings, The Malahat Review, The Nation, New American Review No. 6, Occident, Open Places, The Outsider, Partisan Review, Quarterly Review of Literature, Stony Brook, Sumac.* "A Tree Telling of Orpheus" was first published by the Black Sparrow Press, Los Angeles, California. "A Marigold from North Vietnam" was first published by Albondocani Press, New York. "Snail" was first published by Cloud Marauder Press, Berkeley, California. "Wind Song," "What Wild Dawns," "Secret Festival," "September Moon" were first published in a pamphlet by Walter Hamady, Detroit, Michigan. "An Interim," "Invocation," and "Wings of a God" were first published by *Poetry*. "Embroideries I" and "II" have been published by Black Sparrow Press, Los Angeles, California.

Manufactured in the United States of America

First published as New Directions Paperbook 290 in 1970
Published simultaneously in Canada
by McClelland & Stewart, Limited

New Directions Books are published for James Laughlin
by New Directions Publishing Corporation,
333 Sixth Avenue, New York 10014

Contents

ELEGIES

Dreamed the thong of my sandal broke.
Nothing to hold it to my foot.
How shall I walk?
                    Barefoot?
The sharp stones, the dirt. I would
hobble.
And—
Where was I going?
Where was I going I can't
go to now, unless hurting?
Where am I standing, if I'm
to stand still now?

Because in Vietnam the vision of a Burning Babe
is multiplied, multiplied,
               the flesh on fire
not Christ's, as Southwell saw it, prefiguring
the Passion upon the Eve of Christmas,

but wholly human and repeated, repeated,
infant after infant, their names forgotten,
their sex unknown in the ashes,
set alight, flaming but not vanishing,
not vanishing as his vision but lingering,

cinders upon the earth or living on
moaning and stinking in hospitals three abed;

because of this my strong sight,
my clear caressive sight, my poet's sight I was given
that it might stir me to song,
is blurred.
            There is a cataract filming over
my inner eyes. Or else a monstrous insect
has entered my head, and looks out
from my sockets with multiple vision,

seeing not the unique Holy Infant
burning sublimely, an imagination of redemption,
furnace in which souls are wrought into new life,
but, as off a beltline, more, more senseless figures aflame.

And this insect (who is not there—
it is my own eyes do my seeing, the insect
is not there, what I see is there)
will not permit me to look elsewhere,

or if I look, to see except dulled and unfocused
the delicate, firm, whole flesh of the still unburned.

4

i

Twenty years, forty years, it's nothing.
Not a mirage; the blink
of an eyelid.

Life is nibbling us with little
lips, circling our knees, our
shoulders.
                    What's the difference,
a kiss or a fin-caress. Only sometimes
the water reddens,
we ebb.

Birth, marriage, death, we've had them,
checked them off on our list,
and still stand here

tiptoe on the mud,
half-afloat,
water up to the neck.

It's a big pond.

ii

What do I know?
                    Swing of the
                    birch catkins,
                    drift of
                    watergrass,
                    tufts of
                    green on the
                    trees,

5

(flowers, not leaves,
bearing intricately
little winged seeds
to fly in fall)
and whoever
I meet now,
on the path.
It's not enough.

iii

Biology and the computer—
the speaker implies
we're obsolescent,

we who grew up
towards utopias.

In this
amnesia of the heart
I'm wondering,

I almost believe him.
What do I know?
A poem, turn of the head,

some certainty
of mordant delight—
five notes, the return
of the All Day Bird—:

truces, for the new moon
or the spring solstice,
and at midnight the firing resumes,

far away.
It's not real.

We wanted
more of our life to live in us.
To imagine each other.

iv

Twenty years, forty years,
'to live in the present' was a utopia
moved towards

in tears, stumbling, falling,
getting up, going on—
and now the arrival,

the place of pilgrimage curiously
open, not, it turns out,
a circle of holy stones,

no altar, no
high peak,
no deep valley, the world's navel,

but a plain,
only green tree-flowers
thinly screening the dayglare

and without silence—
we hear the traffic, the highway's
only a stonesthrow away.

Is this the place?

v

This is not the place.
The spirit's left it.

7

Back to that mud my feet felt
when as a child I fell off a bridge
and almost drowned, but rising

found myself dreamily upright,
water sustaining me,
my hair watergrass.

vi

Fishes bare their teeth to our flesh.
The sky's drifting toward our mouths.
Forty years redden the spreading circles.
Blink of an eyelid,
nothing,
obsolete future—

vii

If I should find my poem is deathsongs.
If I find it has ended, when
I looked for the next step.

Not Spring is unreal to me,
I have the tree-flowers by heart.
Love, twenty years, forty years, my life,
        is unreal to me.
I love only the stranger
coming to meet me now
up the path that's pinpricked with
yellow fallen crumbs of pollen.

I who am not about to die,
I who carry my life about with me openly,
health excellent, step light, cheerful, hungry,

my starwheel rolls. Stops
on the point of sight.
Reduced to an eye
I forget what
                 I
was.

Asking the cold spring
what if my poem is deathsongs.

for B. and H. F.

Yes, he is here in this
open field, in sunlight, among
the few young trees set out
to modify the bare facts—

he's here, but only
because we are here.
When we go, he goes with us

to be your hands that never
do violence, your eyes
that wonder, your lives

that daily praise life
by living it, by laughter.

He is never alone here,
never cold in the field of graves.

While we were visiting David's grave
I saw at a little distance

a woman hurrying towards another grave
hands outstretched, stumbling

in her haste; who then
fell at the stone she made for

and lay sprawled upon it, sobbing,
sobbing and crying out to it.

She was neatly dressed in a pale coat
and seemed neither old nor young.

I couldn't see her face, and my friends
seemed not to know she was there.

Not to distress them, I said nothing.
But she was not an apparition.

And when we walked
back to the car in silence

I looked stealthily back and saw she rose
and quieted herself and began slowly

to back away from the grave.
Unlike David, who lives

in our lives, it seemed
whoever she mourned dwelt

there, in the field, under stone.
It seemed the woman

believed whom she loved heard her,
heard her wailing, observed

the nakedness of her anguish,
and would not speak.

Tenebrae

(Fall of 1967)

Heavy, heavy, heavy, hand and heart.
We are at war,
bitterly, bitterly at war.

And the buying and selling
buzzes at our heads, a swarm
of busy flies, a kind of innocence.

Gowns of gold sequins are fitted,
sharp-glinting. What harsh rustlings
of silver moiré there are,
to remind me of shrapnel splinters.

And weddings are held in full solemnity
not of desire but of etiquette,
the nuptial pomp of starched lace;
a grim innocence.

And picnic parties return from the beaches
burning with stored sun in the dusk;
children promised a TV show when they get home
fall asleep in the backs of a million station wagons,
sand in their hair, the sound of waves
quietly persistent at their ears.
They are not listening.

Their parents at night
dream and forget their dreams.
They wake in the dark
and make plans. Their sequin plans
glitter into tomorrow.
They buy, they sell.

13

They fill freezers with food.
Neon signs flash their intentions
into the years ahead.

And at their ears the sound
of the war. They are
not listening, not listening.

The Gulf

(*During the Detroit Riots, 1967*)

Far from our garden at the edge of a gulf,
where we calm our nerves in the rain,

(scrabbling a little in earth to pull weeds
and make room for transplants—

dirt under the nails, it
hurts, almost, and yet feels good)

far from our world the heat's on.
Among the looters a boy of eleven

grabs from a florist's showcase (the *Times* says)
armfuls of gladioli, all he can carry,

and runs with them. What happens?
I see him

dart into a dark entry where there's no one
(the shots, the shouting, the glass smashing

heard dully as traffic is heard).
Breathless he halts to examine

the flesh of dream: he squeezes
the strong cold juicy stems, long as his legs,

tries the mild leafblades—they don't cut.
He presses his sweating face

into flower faces, scarlet and pink and purple,
white and blood red, smooth, cool—his heart is **pounding.**

15

But all at once an absence
makes itself known to him—it's like

a hole in the lungs,
life running out. They are without

perfume!
          Cheated, he drops them.
White men's flowers.

They rustle in falling,
lonely he stands there, the sheaves

cover his sneakered feet . . .
                    There's no place to go
with or without his prize.

Far away, in our garden he cannot imagine,
I'm watching to see if he picks up the flowers

at last or goes,
leaving them lie.

But nothing happens.
He stands there.

He goes on standing there,
useless knowledge in my mind's eye.

Nothing will move him.
We'll live out our lives

in our garden on the edge of a gulf,
and he in the hundred years' war ten heartbeats long

unchanging among the dead flowers,
no place to go.

i

Biafra. Biafra. Biafra.
Small stock of compassion
grown in us by the imagination
(when we would let it) and by
photos of napalmed children and by
the voice of Thich Nath Hanh
has expended itself, saying
Vietnam, Vietnam: trying
to end that war.
           Now we look sluggishly
at photos of children dying in Biafra: dully
accumulate overdue statistics: Massacre
of the Ibos: Do nothing: The poisoning
called 'getting used to'
has taken place: we are
the deads: no room
for love in us: what's left over
changes to bile, brims over: stain on the cushion:
And the news from Biafra (doesn't make the headlines,
not in today's paper at all)
doesn't even get in past our eyes.

ii

Biafra, Biafra, Biafra.
Hammering the word against my breast:
trying to make room for more knowledge
in my bonemarrow:
And all I see
is coarse faces grinning, painted by Bosch
on TV screen as Humphrey
gets nominated: then, flash,

patient sadness,
eyes in a skull: photo
of Biafran boy (age 5?)
            sitting down to die:
And know
no hope: Don't know
what to do: Do nothing:

At any moment the heart
breaks for nothing—

poor folk got up in their best,
rich ones trying, trying to please—

each touch and a new fissure appears,
such a network, I think of an old
china pie-plate
left too long in the oven.

If on the bloody muscle its namesake
patiently pumping in the thoracic cavity

each flick of fate incised itself,
who'd live long? —but this beats on

in the habit of minute response,
with no gift for the absolute.

Disasters
of history weigh on it, anguish

of mortality presses
in on its sides

but neither crush it to dust nor
split it apart. What

is under the cracked glaze?

For Paul and Sally Goodman

Between waking and sleeping I saw my life
in the form of an egg made of colored stones,
half-made, yet the dome of it implied
by the built-up set and curve of the mosaic.
Star stones, lozenges, triangles, irregular pebbles,
brilliants and amber, granite and veined chips of
dark rock, glints of silver and fool's gold and gold;
and each was the sign of someone I had known,
                              from whose life
of presence or word my soul's form,
egg of my being,
had taken its nourishment and grown.

Life yet unlived was space defined
by that base of uncountable, varied fragments,
each unique but all fitting close,
shining or somber, curve meeting curve, or angle
laid next to angle with unpredictable precision
—except in one place: and there a gap was,
a little hole, an emptiness
among the chips and flakes of spirit-stone.
It was a life missing that might have touched mine,
a person, Mathew Ready,
now never to be known, my soul-egg
always to be incomplete for lack of one
spark of sapphire gone from the world.

20

i

While the war drags on, always worse,
the soul dwindles sometimes to an ant
rapid upon a cracked surface;

lightly, grimly, incessantly
it skims the unfathomed clefts where despair
seethes hot and black.

ii

Children in the laundromat
waiting while their mothers fold sheets.
A five-year-old boy addresses
a four-year-old girl. 'When I say,
Do you want some gum? say *yes.*'
'Yes . . .' 'Wait!—Now:
Do you want some gum?'
'Yes!' 'Well yes means no,
so you can't have any.'
He chews. He pops a big, delicate bubble at her.

O language, virtue
of man, touchstone
worn down by what
gross friction . . .

                And,
' "It became necessary
to destroy the town to save it,"
a United States major said today.
He was talking about the decision
by allied commanders to bomb and shell the town
regardless of civilian casualties,
to rout the Vietcong.'

21

O language, mother of thought,
are you rejecting us as we reject you?

Language, coral island
accrued from human comprehensions,
human dreams,

you are eroded as war erodes us.

iii

To repossess our souls we fly
to the sea. To be reminded
of its immensity, and the immense sky
in which clouds move at leisure,
transforming their lives ceaselessly,
sternly, playfully.

Today is the 65th day since de Courcy Squire, war-resister,
began her fast in jail. She is 18.

And the sun
is warm bread, good to us, honest.
And the sand gives itself to our feet
or to our outstretched bodies,
hospitable, accommodating, its shells
unendingly at hand for our wonder.

. . . arrested with 86 others Dec. 7. Her crime:
sitting down in front of a police wagon
momentarily preventing her friends from being
hauled to prison. Municipal Judge Heitzler
handed out 30-day suspended sentences to several others
accused of the same offense, but condemned
Miss Squire to 8 months in jail and fined her
$650. She had said in court 'I don't think there should be
roles like judge and defendant.'

iv

Peace as grandeur. Energy
serene and noble. The waves
break on the packed sand,

butterflies take the cream o' the foam,
from time to time a palmtree lets fall
another dry branch, calmly.
                        The restlessness
of the sound of waves
transforms itself in its persistence
to that deep rest.
                        At fourteen
after measles my mother took me
to stay by the sea. In the austere presence

of Beachy Head we sat long hours
close to the tideline. She read aloud
from George Eliot, while I half-dozed
and played with pebbles. Or I read
to myself Richard Jefferies'
The Story of My Heart, which begins

in such majesty.
                        I was mean and grouchy
much of the time, but she forgave me,

and years later remembered
only the peace of that time.

The quiet there is
in listening.
                        Peace could be

that grandeur, that dwelling
in majestic presence, attuned
to the great pulse.

The cocks crow all night
far and near. Hoarse with expectation.
And by day stumble red-eyed in the dust
where the heat flickers its lizard tongue.

In my dream the city
was half Berlin, half Chicago—
midwest German, Cincinnati perhaps,
where de Courcy Squire is.
There were many of us
jailed there, in moated fortresses—
five of them, with monosyllabic
guttural names. But by day
they led us through the streets,
dressed in our prisoners' robes—
smocks of brown holland—
and the people watched us pass
and waved to us, and gave us
serious smiles of hope.

Between us and the beach
a hundred yards of trees, bushes, buildings,
cut the breeze. But at the *verge*
of the salt flood, always
a steady wind, prevailing.

While we await your trial,
(and this is no dream) we are

free to come and go. To rise
from sleep and love and dreams about
ambiguous circumstance, and from
waking in darkness to cockcrow, and moving
deliberately (by keeping still) back into
morning sleep; to rise and float

24

into the blue day, the elaborate rustlings
of the palmtrees way overhead; to hover
with black butterflies at the lemon-blossom.
The sea awaits us; there are sweet oranges
on our plates; the city grayness has been
washed off our skins, we take pleasure
in each other's warmth of rosy brown.

vi

'Puerto Rico, Feb. 23, 1968.

                         . . . Some people, friends sincerely
concerned for us but who don't seem to understand what
it's really all about, apparently feel sorry for us because
Mitch has been indicted. One letter this morning said,
shyly and abruptly, after talking about quite unrelated mat-
ters, "My heart aches for you." Those people don't understand that however boring the trial will be in some ways,
and however much of a distraction, as it certainly is, from
the things one's nature would sooner be engaged with, yet
it's quite largely a kind of pleasure too, a relief, a satisfac-
tion of the need to confront the war-makers and, in the
process, do something to wake up the bystanders.
    . . . Mitch and the others have a great deal of support,
people who think of them as spokesmen; they have good
lawyers, and have had and will have a lot of publicity of the
kind one hopes will be useful—I don't mean useful for their
case, saving them from going to jail, I mean useful towards
clarifying the issues, stopping the draft, helping to end the
war.'

    But something like a cramp
    of fury begins to form

(in the blue day, in the sweetness
of life we float in, allowed
this interim before the trial)
a cramp of fury at the mild,
saddened people whose hearts ache
not for the crimes of war,
the unspeakable—of which, then,
I won't speak—
and not for de Courcy Squire's
solitary passion
                but for us.

Denied visitors, even her parents;
confined to a locked cell without running water
or a toilet.
              On January 29th, the 53rd day of her fast,
Miss Squire was removed to a hospital.
All the doctors would do was inform her that
the fast may cause her permanent brain injury.

'The sympathy of mild good folk,
a kind of latex from their leaves;
our inconvenience draws it out.

The white of egg without the yolk,
it soothes their conscience and relieves
the irritations of their doubt.

. . . You see how it is—I am angry that they feel no outrage.
Their feeling flows in the wrong directions and at the wrong
intensity. And all I can bring forth out of my anger is a
few flippant rhymes. What I want to tell you—no, not you,
you understand it; what I want them to grasp is that though
I understand that Mitch may have to go to jail and that it
will be a hard time for him and for me, yet, because it's for

26

doing what we know we must do, that hardship is imagi-
nable, encompassable, and a small thing in the face of the
slaughter in Vietnam and the other slaughter that will come.
And there is no certainty he will go to jail.'

And the great savage saints of outrage—
who have no lawyers,
who have no interim
in which to come and go,
for whom there is no world left—
their bodies rush upon the air in flames,
sparks fly, fragments of charred rag
spin in the whirlwind, a vacuum
where there used to be this monk or that,
Norman Morrison, Alice Hertz.

Maybe they are crazy. I know I could never
bring myself to injure my own flesh, deliberately.
And there are other models of behavior
to aspire to—A. J. Muste did not burn himself
but worked through a long life to make from outrage
islands of compassion others could build on.
Dennis Riordon, Bob Gilliam, how many others,
are alive and free in the jails. Their word is good,
language draws breath again in their *yes* and *no*,
true testimony of love and resistance.

But we need
the few who could bear no more,
who would try anything,
who would take the chance
that their deaths among the uncountable
masses of dead might be real to those who
don't dare imagine death.
Might burn through the veil that blinds
those who do not imagine the burned bodies
of other people's children.

We need them.
Brands that flare to show us
the dark we are in,
to keep us moving in it.

vii

To expand again, to plunge
our dryness into the unwearying source—

but not to forget.
Not to forget but to remember better.

We float in the blue day
darkly. We rest behind half-closed louvers,
the hot afternoon clouds up,
the palms hold still.

'I have a medical problem that can be cured'—
Miss Squire said last week when she was removed
from the city workhouse to Cincinnati General Hospital,
'I have a medical problem that can be cured
only by freedom.'

Puerto Rico, February–March, 1968

28

What wild dawns there were
    in our first years here
when we would run outdoors naked
to pee in the long grass behind the house
        and see over the hills such streamers,
        such banners of fire and blue (the blue
        that is Lilith to full day's honest Eve)—
What feathers of gold under the morning star
    we saw from dazed eyes before
stumbling back to bed chilled with dew
to sleep till the sun was high!

Now if we wake early
    we don't go outdoors—or I don't
    and you if you do go
    rarely call me to see the day break.
I watch the dawn through glass: this year
        only cloudless flushes of light, paleness
        slowly turning to rose,
        and fading subdued.
We have not spoken of these tired
risings of the sun.

FOUR EMBROIDERIES

Rose Red's hair is brown as fur
and shines in firelight as she prepares
supper of honey and apples, curds and whey,
for the bear, and leaves it ready
on the hearth-stone.

Rose White's grey eyes
look into the dark forest.

Rose Red's cheeks are burning,
sign of her ardent, joyful
compassionate heart.
Rose White is pale,
turning away when she hears
the bear's paw on the latch.

When he enters, there is
frost on his fur,
he draws near to the fire
giving off sparks.

Rose White catches the scent of the forest,
of mushrooms, of rosin.

Together Rose Red and Rose White
sing to the bear;
it is a cradle song, a loom song,
a song about marriage, about
a pilgrimage to the mountains
long ago.
           Raised on an elbow,
the bear stretched on the hearth
nods and hums; soon he sighs
and puts down his head.

33

He sleeps; the Roses
bank the fire.
Sunk in the clouds of their feather bed
they prepare to dream.

Rose Red in a cave that smells of honey
dreams she is combing the fur of her cubs
with a golden comb.
Rose White is lying awake.

Rose White shall marry the bear's brother.
Shall he too
when the time is ripe,
step from the bear's hide?
Is that other, her bridegroom,
here in the room?

An Embroidery   (II)

(from Andrew Lang and H. J. Ford)

It was the name's music drew me first:
Catherine and her Destiny.
And some glow of red gold, of bronze,
I knew there—glint from the fire
          in a great hearth   awakening
the auburn light in her hair
         and in the heaped-up treasure
weighed in the balance.
                  The events
were blent in this light,
out of sequence.

But always
there seemed a flaw in the tale as told.
If, as it said, she chose sorrow in youth,
what power would she have to welcome joy
         when it came at last to her worn hands,
         her body broken on Destiny's strange little wheel?
How could she take pleasure, when grief was a habit,
in the caprice of a cruel King's making her Queen?
And my Catherine, who would have chosen joy at once,
now while her hair sparked as she brushed it
   and her face was already sad with beauty's sadness
   and had no need for the marks of care—
         (yes, surely she did choose so:
             the tale as told breaks down, grows
                    vague)
—how she laughed when she found her Destiny
         tucked under seven quilts of down,
laughed at the ball of silk
held out impatiently by those fingers of bone,
all that power half asleep on the cloudy mountain!

35

Catherine threw down her cloak on Destiny's bed
for an eighth coverlid,
and merrily took the thread,
stepped out of her youth's brocade slippers
           and set out barefoot, strong from her years of
                                            pleasure,
           to wander the roads of the second half of her life.

An Embroidery   (III) Red Snow

(*after one of the* Parables from
Nature *by Mrs. Gatty*)

Crippled with desire, he questioned it.
Evening upon the heights, juice of the pomegranate:
who could connect it with sunlight?

He took snow into his
red from cold hands.
It would not acknowledge the blood inside,
stayed white, melted only.

And all summer, beyond how many plunging valleys,
                              remote, verdant lesser peaks,
still there were fields
                    by day silver,
                        hidden often in thunderheads,
but faithful before night, crimson.
He knew it was red snow.

He grows tall, and sets out.
The story, inexorably, is of arrival long after, by dark.
Tells he stood waiting
                bewildered
                    in stinging silver towards dawn,
                    and looked over abysses, back:

        the height of his home, snowy, red,
        taunted him.   Fable snuffs out.
                                What did he do?

                    He grew old.
                        With bloodbright hands he wrought
                    icy monuments.
                Beard and long hair flying he rode the whirlwind,
keening the praises of red snow.

(after a lost poem, 1947)

Lost wooden poem,
cows and people wending
downmountain slowly
to wooden homesteads

cows first, the families
following calmly their swaying,
their pausing, their moving ahead in dreamy
constancy.
Children asleep in arms of old men,
healthy pallor of smooth cheeks facing
back to high pastures left for the day,
are borne down as the light
waits to leave.

Upper air glows with motes color of hay,
deep valley darkens.
Lost poem, I know
the cows were fragrant
and sounds were of hooves and feet on earth,
of clumps of good grass torn off, to chew
slowly; and not much talk.
They were returning
to wooden buckets, to lantern-beams
crisp as new straw.

Swiss cheese with black bread,
meadow, wood walls, what

did I do with you, I'm looking
through holes, in cheese, or
pine knotholes, and

who were those peaceful folk, the poem
was twenty years ago, I need it now.

WANTING THE MOON

The beating of the wings.
Unheard.
> The beat rising from dust
> of gray streets
> as now off pale fields.

'A huge crowd of
friends and well-wishers . . .'
> > Someone
figureskates brilliantly
across the lacquer lid of a box
where dreams are stored.
Something
> has to give.

The wings unheard
> > felt as a rush of air,
> of air withdrawn, the breath
taken—
> The blow falls,
> feather and bone
> > stone-heavy.
I am felled,
> rise up
> with changed vision,
a singing in my ears.

41

Not the moon. A flower
on the other side of the water.

The water sweeps past in flood,
dragging a whole tree by the hair,

a barn, a bridge. The flower
sings on the far bank.

Not a flower, a bird calling,
hidden among the darkest trees, music

over the water, making a silence
out of the brown folds of the river's cloak.

The moon. No, a young man walking
under the trees.   There are lanterns

among the leaves.
Tender, wise, merry,

his face is awake with its own light,
I see it across the water as if close up.

A jester.   The music rings from his bells,
gravely, a tune of sorrow,

I dance to it on my riverbank.

Not to Have . . .

Not to have but to be.
The black heart of the poppy,
O to lie there as seed.

To become the belovéd.
As the world ends, to enter
the last note of its music.

Wanting the Moon   (II)

Not the moon.   To be a bronze head
inhabited by a god.
          A torso of granite
left out in the weather ten thousand years,
adored by passing clouds.
Their shadows painting it, brushstrokes of dust blue.
Giving themselves to it in infinite rain.
          To be a cloud. Sated with wandering, seize
the gaiety of change from within, of dissolution,
of raining.
          To lie down in the dreams
of a young man whose hair
is the color of mahogany.

43

A Cloak

*'For there's more enterprise
In walking naked.'*
                    W. B. Yeats

And I walked naked
from the beginning

breathing in
my life,
breathing out
poems,

arrogant in innocence.

But of the song-clouds my breath made
in cold air

a cloak has grown,
white and,
            where here a word
            there another
froze, glittering,
stone-heavy.

A mask I had not meant
to wear, as if of frost,
covers my face.
            Eyes looking out,
a longing silent at song's core.

Wanted
to give away pride,
like donating one oil well when you know
you own a whole delta.

Gave away nothing: no takers.
The derricks are idle.

Punt through the shallows,
pushing fat lilies aside,
my shadow,
            in your dark boat.

Craving

Wring the swan's neck, seeking
a little language of drops of blood.

How can we speak of blood, the sky
is drenched with it.

A little language
of dew, then.

It dries.

A language
of leaves underfoot.
Leaves on the tree, trembling
in speech. Poplars
            tremble and speak
if you draw near them.

45

Swan that sings and
        does not die.
Aimless, the long neck stretched out,
the note held, death
withheld.   Wings
creaking in strong flight,
not,
    not giving way,
weary of strength

        the music
ending without conclusion

Earth Dust

So slowly I am dying
you wouldn't know it.
They say birth begins it.
                But for three decades, four,
        the sky's valves lie open,
           or close to open over again,
a green pearl revealed.

Slowly, slowly,
I spin towards the sun.

I am waiting.
On benches, at the corners
of earth's waitingrooms,
by trees whose sap rises, rises
to escape in gray leaves and lose
itself in the last air.
Waiting
for who comes at last,
late, lost, the forever
longed-for, walking
not my road but crossing
the corner where I wait.

Someone imagined
who was real too

and did not want me to
imagine him,
to violate

his dream of himself.

. . . .

The touch of dream
upon the fine white

skin of someone caught
in someone else's imagined life.

Nails of imagination
tenderly scratching the back of

someone who isn't there,
who's there heavy-hearted,

and won't look up.

. . . .

Who won't look up to enter
the dream that violates
his imagined order.

Gently, insistently,
re-entering
the order of himself,

inviolate dream,
unimagined.

48

My madness is dear to me.
I who was almost always the sanest among my friends,
one to whom others came for comfort,
now at my breasts (that look timid and ignorant,
        that don't look as if milk had flowed from them,
        years gone by)
cherish a viper.
          Hail, little serpent of useless longing
that may destroy me,
that bites me with such idle
needle teeth.

I who am loved by those who love me
for honesty,
to whom life was an honest breath
          taken in good faith,
I've forgotten how to tell joy from bitterness.

Dear to me, dear to me,
blue poison, green pain in the mind's veins.
How am I to be cured against my will?

'My soul's a black boy with a long way to go.
a long way to know if black is beautiful.'
'But doesn't your soul fly, don't you know who you are?'

'Flies, has flown, yes, poems and praise
known to it—but like a worn kite, old silk
mended with paper,
                        bucks the wind, falters, leans
sideways, is falling.'
                        'And you spoke of it
as a boy?'
            'That boy with long, cold
stems of stolen gladioli aching his arms:
No place to go.'

Black beans, white sunlight.
These have sufficed.

Approval of mothers, of brothers,
of strangers—a plunge of the hands
in sifted flour, over the wrists.
It gives pleasure.

And being needed. Being loved for that.
Being forgiven.

What mountains there are
to border solitude and provide
limits, blue or
dark as raisins.

But hunger: a hunger there is
refuses. Refuses the earth.

A stealth in air that means:

the swallows have flown
south while I flew
north again.

Still, in the quiet there are
chickadees,
to make me grudgingly smile,
and crickets curious about
my laundry put out to bleach
on brown grass.

So I do smile.
What else to do?
Melancholy is boring.

And if the well goes dry—
and it has;
and if the body-count goes up—
and it does;
and if the summer spent
itself before I took it
into my life—?

Nothing to do but take
crumbs that fall from the chickadee's table
—or starve.
But the time for starving is not yet.

Up the long street of castles, over cobbles
we rode at twilight, alone.

Harlech, Duino, Azay-le-Rideau,
and many more,

neighboring one another.
Of all the windows

none were lit. The sky shone
in some, pale.

Through silence moved
the creak of saddles, jingle of gear.
Uphill,

though not very steep,
the road lay, and was white.

High stepped the horses' feet.

But as I woke I saw I could not see
who that belovéd was that rode with me.

No reason: hyacinthine, ordinary,
extraordinary, creature:

on your two legs, running,
the grey brain above
transmitting its poetry—

just that you are, man, someone,
wings at your heels, the gods sent

to tell me.

Adam's Complaint

Some people,
no matter what you give them,
still want the moon.

The bread,
the salt,
white meat and dark,
still hungry.

The marriage bed
and the cradle,
still empty arms.

You give them land,
their own earth under their feet,
still they take to the roads.

And water: dig them the deepest well,
still it's not deep enough
to drink the moon from.

Trying to remember old dreams. A voice. Who came in.
And meanwhile the rain, all day, all evening,
quiet steady sound. Before it grew too dark
I watched the blue iris leaning under the rain,
the flame of the poppies guttered and went out.
A voice. Almost recalled. There have been times
the gods entered. Entered a room, a cave?
A long enclosure where I was, the fourth wall of it
too distant or too dark to see. The birds are silent,
no moths at the lit windows. Only a swaying rosebush
pierces the table's reflection, raindrops gazing from it.
There have been hands laid on my shoulders.
                What has been said to me,
        how has my life replied?
The rain, the rain . . .

Two fading red spots mark on my thighs
where a flea from the fur of a black, curly, yearning dog
bit me, casually, and returned into the fur.

Melanie was the dog's name. That afternoon
she had torn the screen from a door and littered fragments
of screen everywhere, and of chewed-up paper,

stars, whole constellations of paper, glimmered
in shadowy floor corners. She had been punished, adequately;
this was not a first offense. And forgiven,

but sadly: her master knew she would soon discover
other ways to show forth her discontent, her black humor.
Meanwhile, standing on hind legs like a human child,

she came to lean her body, her arms and head,
in my lap. I was a friendly stranger. She gave me
a share of her loneliness, her warmth, her flea.

THE SINGER

Between chores—
                    hulling strawberries,
                    answering letters—
or between poems,

returning to the mirror
to see if I'm there.

Plié, the knees bend,
a frog flexing to spring;
grand battement, the taut leg
flails as if to beat
chaff from the wheat;
attitude, Hermes brings
ambiguous messages
and moves dream-smoothly
yet with hidden strain
that breaks in sweat,
into *arabesque* that traces
swan-lines on vision's stone
that the dancer not seeing
herself, feels in the bone.
Coupé, the air is cut
out from under the foot,
grand jeté, glissade, grand jeté, glissade,
the joy of leaping, of moving by
leaps and bounds, of gliding
to leap, and gliding
to leap becomes, while it lasts,
heart pounding, breath hurting,
the deepest, the only joy.

Where there is violet in the green of the sea
the eye rests, knowing
a depth there.
In the depth where the violet changes, the sea
surrenders to the eye
a knowledge.
Where the blue of shadow rests upon green the sea
knows desire, sorrow
becomes joy
where there is violet in the eye of the sea.
In the changing
depth of desire
the I knows it is open, the distant sea
withholds nothing, surrenders
nothing,
save to the eye. Rests in the sea
desire of joy,
heart's
sorrow. Where there is violet in the green of thc sca.

Whó am I? Whó am I?
It is the old cry wandering in the wind
and with it interwoven
words of reply: I am fiery ember, dispersed
in innumerable fragments
flying in the wind, gray cinders
and black, and all still burning, all bearing
a point of flame
hidden in ashes. Flying upon the nameless
winds and upon those that men
know and name: sirocco,
bise, northeaster, tramontana. I die and again
life is breathed
into me. Whó am I? Whó am I?
My dust burns
in the past and flies before me
into the whirling future,
the Old World, the New World, my soul is scattered
across the continents
in the named places and the named and unnamed
shadowy faces, my years
a hearth from which the sparks wander
and to its stones
blow back at random upon the winds
to kindle the brand again that fades and flares.

Black,
       shining with a yellowish
       dew,
erect,
       revealed by the laughing
       glance of Krishna's eyes:
the terrible lotus.

Topmost leaves of young oak,
        young maple,
            are red—a delicate red
almost maroon.

I am not young,
        and not yet old. Young enough not to be able
            to imagine my own old age. Something in me

puts out new leaves that are red also,
        delicate, fantastic, in June,
            early summer, late spring in the north.

A dark time we live in. One would think
        there would be no summer. No red leaves.
            One would think there would be

no drawings-up of the blind at morning
        to a field awake with flowers.
            Yet with my tuft of new leaves

it is that field I wake to,
        a woman foolish with desire.

Along the tracks
counting
always the right foot awarded
       the tie to step on
the left stumbling all the time in cinders

towards where
    an old caboose
samples of paint were once tried out on
is weathering in a saltmarsh
        to tints Giotto dreamed.

'Shall we
ever reach it?'   'Look—
the tracks take a curve.
We may
      come round to it
if we keep going.'

Somehow nineteen years ago
        clumsily passionate
I drew into me the seed
of a man—
            and bore it, cast it out—

man-seed that grew
                    and became a person
                    whose subtle mind and quick heart

            though I beat him, hurt him,
            while I fed him, loved him,

now stand beyond me, out in the world
                                beyond my skin
beautiful and strange as if
        I had given birth to a tree.

A Marigold from North Vietnam

for Barbara Deming

Marigold   resurrection flower
that the dead   love and come forth
by candlelight to inhale
scent of   sharp   a smoke-of-watchfires
odor.   The living
taste it as if   on the tongue
acrid.   In summer it tells   of fall
in fall   of winter   in winter
of spring.   The leaves
very fine   delicate.   The flowers
petal-crowded   long-lasting.
Drooping in dryness   the whole plant
in minutes   lifts itself   resilient
given water.   The earth in the pot was dug
in quick kindness   by moonlight   for gift
in Maine   but to the root-threads cling still
some crumbs of Vietnam.   When I water
the marigold these too   are moistened
and give forth   nourishment.

How easy it is to return
into the great nowhere!

Two weeks incommunicado
on the border of somebody else's life
equals two months at sea.

Whom did I anciently
pine for? What were my passions?

The plains of the sea
modulate quiet songs that light
hums to itself.
                    The decks
are holystoned. Smoothly
the ship makes way, no shoreline
to mark her passage.

The wake fading.
Translated.

If even so I tremble sometimes,
if I scan the horizon for land-shadow;

it is because I am so unused
to the sufficiency of
random essentials:

moon, box, marigold, *Two Hundred and One
French Verbs.*

I practise breathing, my spirit acquires
color and texture of unbleached linen.

I am unused to
the single ocean,
the one moon.

Secret Festival; September Moon

Pandemonium of owls
plying from east to west and
west to east, over the full-moon sea of
mown grass.
                    The low-voiced
and the wailing high-voiced
hooting together, neither in dialogue
                    nor in unison,
                              an overlapping
antiphonal a fox
                    barks to,
as if to excel, whose obligato
the owls ignore.
They raise
the roof of the dark; ferocious
          their joy in the extreme silver
                    the moon has floated out from itself,
luminous air in which their eyes
don't hurt or close,
                    the night of the year
          their incantations have raised—
          and if
foxes believe it's theirs, there's enough to slip
over and round them, earthlings, of owlish fire.

The moon tiger.
In the room, here.
It came in, it is
prowling sleekly
under and over
the twin beds.
See its small head,
silver smooth,
hear the pad of its
large feet. Look,
its white stripes
in the light that slid
through the jalousies.
It is sniffing our
clothes, its cold nose
nudges our bodies.
The beds are narrow,
but I'm coming in with you.

Crackle and flash almost in the kitchen sink—the
thunderclap follows even as I
jump back frightened,
afraid to touch metal—

> The roofgutters pouring down
> whole rivers, making holes in the earth—
> The electric bulbs fade and go out,
> another thin crackling lights the window
> and in the instant before the next onslaught of kettle-
> drums,

a small bird, I don't know its name,
among the seagreen tossed leaves
> begins its song.

'That creep Tolstoy,' she sobbed.
'He. . . He. . . couldn't even. . .'
Something about his brother dying.

The serfs' punishments
have not ceased to suppurate on their backs.
Woodlots. People. Someone crying

under the yellow
autumn birchgrove drove him
wild: A new set of resolves:

When gambling, that almost obsolete fever,
or three days with the gypsies
sparked him into pure ego, he could,

just the same, write home, 'Sell them.'
It's true. 'Still,' (someone who loved her said,
cold and firm while she dissolved,

hypocrite, in self disgust, *lectrice*)
'Still, he kept on. He wrote
all that he wrote; and seems to have understood

better than most of us:
to be human isn't easy. It's not
easy to be a serf or a master and learn

that art. It takes nerve. Bastard. Fink.
Yet the grief
trudging behind his funeral, he earned.'

My sign!
  —yours, too—
anyone's—
   aloft in the coppery
afterglow, gulls or pigeons,
    too high to tell,
way above downtown highrise
wheeling serene,
     whether to feed or
for flight's sake
    makes no difference
sliding the air's
    mountains,
unhastening

the bows of their winged bodies drawn
sostenuto over the hover of
   smoke, grey gauze tinged with rust:
over the traffic of our lives—a sign
if I look up—
   or you—
anyone.

i

At the dump bullfrogs
converse as usual.
It's their swamp
    below the garbage tip,
where they were masters
long before towns had
dumps.   Rapid
the crossfire of their
utterance.
Their eyes
        are at water level.
Rats prowl
among the soiled bulrushes.
The frogs sound angry.
    But they have not
    hopped away in the time of rains.
    They inhabit their heritage,
    pluck the twilight
                pleasurably.
Are they irascible?
Yes, but not bored.
    It is summer,
    their spirits are high.
Urgently,
    anxiously,
above their glistening heads,
                fireflies
    switch
    on and
          off.

74

ii

The fireflies desperately
entreat their unknown bridegrooms,
their somewhere brides,
            to discover them.
                        Now while there is time.
But what of the moths?
Their lives also are brief,
but hour after hour—
                        their days and years—
they choose to cling upon windows
ingazing to lighted rooms.
Silk of their bodies unruffled,
dust on spread wings unsmirched.

            Their eyes' lamps
            when mens' lights are put out
            glow steadily—they try
            still to look in towards departed splendor
that may return?

            What secret, worth
            this impassioned stillness
is it they dream of?

I want some funny jazz band
      to wake me,
tell me life's been dreaming me.
I want something like love, but made
      all of string or pebbles,
       oboe of torn air
to tear me to my senses.
        Emily's black birds
don't bate their banjos nor the throbbing
      of their quick hearts.
The leaves part to reveal
      more leaves, and darkness,
      darkness and the intense
      poised sequence of leaves.
I want to take the last of all leaves
        between my lips and taste
          its weight of stone.

Burden, grace,
artifice coiled
brittle on my back, integral,

I thought to crawl
out of you,

yearned for the worm's
lowly freedom that can go

under earth and whose
slow arrow pierces
the thick of dark

but in my shell
my life was,

and when I knew it
I remembered

my eyes adept to witness
air and harsh light

and look all ways.

A TREE TELLING OF ORPHEUS

White dawn. Stillness.   When the rippling began
    I took it for sea-wind, coming to our valley with rumors
    of salt, of treeless horizons. But the white fog
didn't stir; the leaves of my brothers remained outstretched,
unmoving.
               Yet the rippling drew nearer—and then
my own outermost branches began to tingle, almost as if
fire had been lit below them, too close, and their twig-tips
were drying and curling.
                      Yet I was not afraid, only
                      deeply alert.

I was the first to see him, for I grew
            out on the pasture slope, beyond the forest.
He was a man, it seemed: the two
moving stems, the short trunk, the two
arm-branches, flexible, each with five leafless
                          twigs at their ends,
and the head that's crowned by brown or gold grass,
bearing a face not like the beaked face of a bird,
         more like a flower's.
                    He carried a burden made of
some cut branch bent while it was green,
strands of a vine tight-stretched across it. From this,
when he touched it, and from his voice
which unlike the wind's voice had no need of our
leaves and branches to complete its sound,
                         came the ripple.
But it was now no longer a ripple (he had come near and
stopped in my first shadow) it was a wave that bathed me
           as if rain
                  rose from below and around me
           instead of falling.
And what I felt was no longer a dry tingling:

81

I seemed to be singing as he sang, I seemed to know
what the lark knows; all my sap
            was mounting towards the sun that by now
                had risen, the mist was rising, the grass
was drying, yet my roots felt music moisten them
deep under earth.

            He came still closer, leaned on my trunk:
            the bark thrilled like a leaf still-folded.
Music! There was no twig of me not
                        trembling with joy and fear.

Then as he sang
it was no longer sounds only that made the music:
he spoke, and as no tree listens I listened, and language
            came into my roots
                        out of the earth,
                into my bark
                        out of the air,
                into the pores of my greenest shoots
                        gently as dew
and there was no word he sang but I knew its meaning.
He told of journeys,
            of where sun and moon go while we stand in dark,
    of an earth-journey he dreamed he would take some day
deeper than roots . . .
He told of the dreams of man, wars, passions, griefs,
            and I, a tree, understood words—ah, it seemed
my thick bark would split like a sapling's that
                        grew too fast in the spring
when a late frost wounds it.

                        Fire he sang,
that trees fear, and I, a tree, rejoiced in its flames.
New buds broke forth from me though it was full summer.
        As though his lyre (now I knew its name)
        were both frost and fire, its chords flamed
up to the crown of me.

I was seed again.
                        I was fern in the swamp.
                                I was coal.

And at the heart of my wood
(so close I was to becoming man or a god)
        there was a kind of silence, a kind of sickness,
                something akin to what men call boredom,
                                                something
(the poem descended a scale, a stream over stones)
                that gives to a candle a coldness
                        in the midst of its burning, he said.

It was then,
                when in the blaze of his power that
                                        reached me and changed me
                I thought I should fall my length,
that the singer began
                        to leave me.   Slowly
                moved from my noon shadow
                                        to open light,
words leaping and dancing over his shoulders
back to me
                rivery sweep of lyre-tones becoming
slowly again
                ripple.

And I
        in terror
                but not in doubt of
                                what I must do
in anguish, in haste,
                wrenched from the earth root after root,
the soil heaving and cracking, the moss tearing asunder—
and behind me the others: my brothers
forgotten since dawn. In the forest
they too had heard,

83

and were pulling their roots in pain
out of a thousand years' layers of dead leaves,
            rolling the rocks away,
                        breaking themselves
                                    out of
                                        their depths.
You would have thought we would lose the sound of the lyre,
                        of the singing
so dreadful the storm-sounds were, where there was no storm,
                no wind but the rush of our
            branches moving, our trunks breasting the air.
            But the music!
                        The music reached us.

Clumsily,
            stumbling over our own roots,
                                rustling our leaves
                                        in answer,
we moved, we followed.

All day we followed, up hill and down.
                        We learned to dance,
for he would stop, where the ground was flat,
                        and words he said
taught us to leap and to wind in and out
around one another   in figures   the lyre's measure designed.
The singer
            laughed till he wept to see us, he was so glad.
                                    At sunset
we came to this place I stand in, this knoll
with its ancient grove that was bare grass then.
            In the last light of that day his song became
farewell.
            He stilled our longing.
            He sang our sun-dried roots back into earth,
watered them: all-night rain of music so quiet

                                    we could almost
              not hear it in the
                          moonless dark.
By dawn he was gone.
                    We have stood here since,
in our new life.
                We have waited.
                              He does not return.
It is said he made his earth-journey, and lost
what he sought.
                It is said they felled him
and cut up his limbs for firewood.
                              And it is said
his head still sang and was swept out to sea singing.
Perhaps he will not return.
                          But what we have lived
comes back to us.
                We see more.
                          We feel, as our rings increase,
something that lifts our branches, that stretches our furthest
                                              leaf-tips
further.
          The wind, the birds,
                          do not sound poorer but clearer,
recalling our agony, and the way we danced.
The music!

RELEARNING THE ALPHABET

I want to give away the warm coat
I bought but found
cold and ungainly.
                    A man's wife will wear it,
          and in exchange the man will tear
an ugly porch off an old empty house,

leave it the way it was,
bare and sightly.

'I am an object to you,' he said.
'My charm, what you call
my charm—
            alien to me.'
'No! No!' she is crying.
'Indissoluble—'The tears hurt her throat.
'—idiosyncratic—you—not an object—'

                (That smiling glance from under
                fair-lashed long lids—complicit—
                :he cannot help it.)

            'Fire of the mind—
your vision—unique—
aware the lynx is there in smoky light,
a god disdained, unrecognized, dragged in darkness
out to sea—'

Fire, light, again,
beginning to dry tears: awaken, illumine.
Pain tears at her with lynx claws
but her throat relaxes.
Still he suspects. (—Not I but your idea
                of who I am.)
                        (Why should he care,
                    not wanting the love I keep holding out
                    stupidly, like a warm coat on a hot day?)

She reflects out loud, 'Aren't all, whom we love,
not *objects*, but—symbols—impersonal—
molten glass in our desire, their dailiness
translucent—?
            The gods in us,
you said: what violence more brutish
than not to see them:

90

I am not doing you
that violence:
                        I see
what is strange in you, and surpasses
with its presence your history . . .'

But she knows the wall is there she can't pass.
The god, the light, the fire,
live in his body she may not touch.
It does not want to touch hers.
Tropism, one of those words she always
had to look up, before its meaning
took root in her, says itself back of her tongue.
She is dark,
                a blackness sinks on her.—*He has*
no tropism towards me, that knowledge.
And yet, and yet, he wants to be known to her,
hungers for love—even from *her* dark source—
        not to pass godlike from form to form, but dig in its
                                                    claws:
even now, love that he does not want.

And he—(he does not say it now, there's nothing
                said now but re-sayings, but it was written already,
                she has the letter)
'You know
better than I
the desolation is gestation. Absence
                                an absolute
                                presence
                                calling forth
                                the person   (the poet)
                        into desperate continuance, toward
                        fragments of light.'

91

Part I

i

Revolution or death. Revolution or death.
Wheels would sing it
                              but railroads are obsolete,
we are among the clouds, gliding, the roar
a toneless constant.
                              Which side are you on?
Revolution, of course. Death is Mayor Daley.
This revolution has no blueprints, and
                      ('What makes this night different
                      from all other nights?')
is the first that laughter and pleasure aren't shot down in.

Life that
              wants to live.
                                    (*Unlived life*
                              of which one can die.)
                      I want the world to go on
                  unfolding. The brain
not gray except in death, the photo I saw
of prismatic radiance pulsing from live tissue.
              I see Dennis Riordon and de Courcy Squire,
              gentle David Worstell, intransigent Chuck Matthei
              blowing angel horns at the imagined corners.
              Jennie Orvino singing
              beatitudes in the cold wind
                          outside a Milwaukee courthouse.
I want their world—in which they already live,
they're not waiting for demolition and reconstruction.
                                    'Begin here.'

Of course I choose
revolution.

ii

And yet, yes, there's the death
that's not the obscene sellout, the coprophiliac spasm
that smears the White House walls with its desensitized
                                                    thumbs.

> Death lovely,
> whispering,
> *a drowsy numbness* . . .
>   *'tis not*
> *from envy of thy happy lot*
>   *lightwingéd dryad* . . .

Even the longest river . . .

Revolution or death. Love
aches me.   . . . *river*
winds somewhere to the sea.

iii

Shining of Lorie's hair, swinging
        alive, color of new copper—

who has died and risen.
'What am I doing here? I had died—'
(The nurses are frightened. The doctor
refuses to tell what happened those four hours.)
whose body at twenty-three is at war
within itself
trying to die again,

whose 'psychic energy' pulls her ten ways:
sculpture   poetry   painting
psychology   photography   teaching
cookery   love   Chinese philosophy
physics

        If she can live I can live.

iv

Trying one corner after another
to flag down a cab
                        at last unthinking as one at last
                        seems to see me,
                                        I run into the traffic—
screech of brakes,
human scream, mine,
anger of drivers and shocked pedestrians
yelling at me!
                Is that how death is,
                that poor, that trivial? I'm
not even frightened, only ashamed,
the driver almost refusing me,
scolding me half the way to the airport, I
strenuous to convince him I'm not
a habitual public danger.
So close to death and thinking only
of being forgiven by strangers.

v

Gliding among clouds.   The will to live
pulses.   Radiant emanations
of living tissue, visible only
to some photo-eye we know
sees true because mind's dream-eye,
inward gage, confirms it.
                Confirmation,
a sacrament.

                Around the Fish
(it's reproduced here in the magazine the air-hostess gives me)
                rearranges itself as *Around the—*
                Nature of Death, is it? *How*
                to Live, What to Do?

after yet another return home,
first thing I see is a picture postcard
that stood on the windowledge all summer,
somehow not seen. An Assyrian relief. The wings
(as I look at the words I've written, 'gliding among clouds')
draw me to pick it up and examine it:
a sturdy muscular being it shows,
thick-bearded, heavy-sandalled;
wings made for crossing from world to world.
His hair is bound with a wreath;
in his left hand he grips
a thickstemmed plant bearing five blossoms.

                                        Who sent him?
I turn the card over—ah! at once
I know the hand—Bill Rose's. This was his message to me,
six months ago, unanswered. Is now the newly dead—
less than three weeks—trying to speak to me
one last time?

          How to live and the will to live,
          what was recalled to me of those
          rainbow pulsations some Russian scientist
          discovered,
          the choosing
          always before me now that sings itself
          quietly, *revolution or death*
                    cluster about some center
                    unknown, shifting but retaining—
                    snowflake forms in a kaleidescope—
                    a character that throughout all transformations
                    reveals them connatural.
                                        And to that cluster
     this winged genie from Nimrud
     now adds himself,
     last sign from a friend whose life
     failed him in some way long before death:

a man my age
a man deeply dissatisfied
as he told me once.

                          'It came on very suddenly; he
found out at the end of the summer that nothing could be
done for him, so to make the waiting easier, he decided to
go on teaching. But within a few weeks of that decision, he
was dead.'
          And someone else writes: 'Mr Rose was such a
lone figure; he lived alone; you mostly saw him alone; and
that's what's so hard to take: he died alone. I never knew
him except by sight.'

          Is there anything
          I write any more that is not
          elegy?
                    Goldengrove
is unleaving all around me; I live
in goldengrove; all day
yesterday and today the air has been filled
with that hesitant downwardness;
the marigolds, the pumpkin, must be sought out
to be seen, the grass
is covered with that cloth, the roads'
margins illuminated.

vi

Learned—not for the first time—my 'roots in the
19th century' put me
                    out of touch.

Born in the '20's, but a late child, my parents' memories
pivoting on their first meeting, Constantinople, 1910, and
returning into the '90's. Reading, I went straight from
Grimm and Andersen to the 19th-century novel. Until the

war—1939—there was a muffin-man who came by in foggy
winter dusks, tea-time, ringing his bell, his wares balanced
on his head according to the mysteries of his trade as if
Dickens were still alive—
The 'Ode to a Nightingale' was the first and only poem I
ever learned by heart. Thus, when I wrote, translating,
'*purged* of legend,' the reader's thought was of Stalin, while
my intention was something more graphic than the literal
'cured'—

and again when I said the sun approached
'to study the flower,' the reader—

       to whom I would give
       all that arms can hold, eyes
       encompass—
alas, thought of a tedious process,
grade-points, term-papers—while I had meant 'study—e.g.,
    I study your face intently
      but its secret eludes me,'
   or, 'he took her hand and studied
   the strong fingers, the veins,
   the curious ring.'

Without a terrain in which, to which, I belong,
language itself is my one home, my Jerusalem,

yet time and the straddled ocean
undo me, maroon me,
(roadblocks, the lines down)—
       I choose
        revolution but my words
often already don't reach forward
       into it—
         (perhaps)

   Whom I would touch
   I may not,

whom I may
I would
but often do not.

My diction marks me
untrue to my time;
change it, I'd be
untrue to myself.
                        I study
a face intently.
Learning.
Beginning to learn.

And while
        I study,
                O, in that act
of passionate attention
A *drowsy numbness*
pains my sense.
                Too happy in thy happiness.
Love of living.   *That wants to live.*   *Unlived life.*
whisper
of goldengrove . . .

Entr'acte

i

Last of October, light thinning
towards the cold. Deep shadow.

Yellow honey, the ridge, a grove 'thrown into relief,'
of tamaracks, lurid, glamorous
upon the breast of
moving darkness, clouds thick with
gunmetal blue.

98

It becomes
November without one's knowing it.
Broad rays from southwest-by-west
single out one by one
the fixed parts of earthscape.

And into the first snowstorm   (marooned)
the lines down
no phone
no lights
no heat
gastank for cooking about to give out
car stuck in the driveway.

        We find candles.
        We light up the woodstove which was all we
        used to have anyway, till a few weeks back.

ii

A fly I thought dead
on its back on the windowsill,
grayed, shrivelled,

slowly waves.
        Yes, what would be its right arm
dreamily moves—out—in—out again
twice, three times.
        It seems
flies dream in dying.

iii

Four p.m.—pleasure
in exercise
in air,

in sound of brook
under and out from
thin ice

pleasure
of chest and shoulders
pushing air that's
not cold enough to hurt.

Jumping
into snowbank—
no sound—

pleasure—

But to the eye
terror of a kind:

black-and-white photo world
not night yet
but at four p.m.
no light we know

hemlock and cedar a toneless black,
snowtufted trunks and boughs
black, sky white, birches
whiter, snow
infinitely whiter: all things
muted: deprived
of color, as if
color were utterance.
A terror
as of eclipse.
The whites graying.

iv

George told me, and then I read it in Beckett,
Proust had a bad memory,
                          the only kind worth having,
Beckett argues: there's no remembrance
                    and so no revelation,
   for those Admirable, terrifying, unimaginable Crichtons
   who don't disremember nothing, keep
   the whole works in mind.
No pain. No sharp stabs of recall. No revelation.

I stretch in luxury; knowledge of the superb badness
of my memory gives me a sense of having thick fur,
a tail, and buried somewhere
a sweet bone, rotten, enticing . . .

What pain! What sharp stabs of recall! What revelations!
The black taste of life, the music
angel tongues buzz when my paws nuzzle it
out into light!

v

Again to hold—'capture' they say—
moments and their processions in palm
of mind's hand.
                    Have you ever,
in stream or sea,
                    felt the silver of fish
pass through your hand-hold? not to stop it,
block it from going onward, but feel it
move in its wave-road?
                    To make
                    of song a chalice,
                         of Time,
                    a communion wine.

101

Part II

Can't go further.
If there's to be a
second part, it's not
a going beyond, I'm
still here.

To dig down,
to re-examine.

. . . .

What is the revolution I'm driven
to name, to live in? —that now roars,
a toneless constant, now
sings itself?

                    It's in the air: no air
                              to breathe without
                    scent of it,
                              pervasive:
                    odor of snow,
                              freshwater,
                                        stink of dank
                              vegetation recomposing.

—Yet crisply
the moon's risen,
full, complete.
Secret uprising (last time I looked,
                    surely not long since,
                    dark was
                    as complete).
The snowfields have been
taken over

(glistening crust of ice upon snow
in driftwaves, curves of stilled
wind-caress, bare to the moon
in silence of adoration).

If it were so for us!
But that's the moon's world.

. . . .

Robert reminds me *revolution*
implies the circular: an exchange
of position, the high
brought low, the low
ascending, a revolving,
an endless rolling of the wheel. The wrong word.
We use the wrong word. A new life
isn't the old life in reverse, negative of the same photo.
But it's the only
word we have . . .

. . . .

Chuck Matthei
travels the country
                a harbinger.
(He's 20. His golden beard was pulled and clipped
        by a Wyoming sheriff, but no doubt has grown
                                        again
        though he can't grow knocked-out teeth.
        He wears sneakers even in winter,
        to avoid animal-hide; etc.)
And on his journeyings bears
my poem 'A Man'
to prisoners in the jails.
            Of Mitch I wrote it,

even before anyone heard
the voice he
brought to song.
                But Chuck has found in it
a message for all who resist war,
                disdain to kill,
                try to equate
                'human' with 'humane.'
(And if his intransigeance
brings us another despair
and we call it 'another form of aggression,'
don't we confess—

                wishing he had a sense of humor—
our own extremity?)

'Living a life' the poem begins.
'—the beauty of deep lines
dug in your cheeks'

                and ends,
'you pick out
your own song from the uproar,

line by line,
and at last throw back
your head and sing it.'
                Next on the mimeograph follows:
'THERE IS ONLY AS MUCH PEACE AS THERE ARE
PEACEFUL PEOPLE'
                (A. J. Muste)
                Then Chuck has written:
This is your only life—live it well!

No one man can bring about a social change—
       but each man's life is a whole and necessary part of his
       society,
       a necessary step in any change,
       and a powerful example of the possibility of life
       for others.

Let all of our words and our actions speak the possibility of
peace and cooperation between men.
Too long have we used the excuse:
'I believe in peace, but that other man does not—when
he lays down his arms, then I will follow.'

Which of us deserves to wait to be the last good man
on earth; how long will we wait if all of us wait?

Let each man begin a one-man revolution of peace and
mutual aid—so that there is at least that much peace . . .
a beginning; . . .

A beginning.
Where shall we
begin?
Can't go
further.
          Time, says the old Canon,
in Denis Saurat's *Death and the Dreamer*,
        is not a sequence,
        as man's simplicity thinks, but radiates
out from a center
            every direction,
            all
             dimensions
               (pulsations, as from living cells,
radiant—

       . . . .

May 14th, 1969—Berkeley
Went with some of my students to work in the People's
Park. There seemed to be plenty of digging and gardening
help so we decided, as Jeff had his truck available, to shovel
up the garbage that had been thrown into the west part of
the lot and take it out to the city dump.

O happiness
in the sun! Is it
that simple, then,
to live?
—crazy rhythm of
scooping up barehanded
(all the shovels already in use)
careless of filth and broken glass
—scooping up garbage together
poets and dreamers studying
joy together, clearing
refuse off the neglected, newly recognized,
humbly waiting ground, place, locus, of what could be our
New World even now, our revolution, one and one and
one and one together, black children swinging, green
guitars, that energy, that music, no one
telling anyone what to do,
everyone doing,

each leaf of
the new grass near us
a new testament . . .

Out to the dump:
acres of garbage glitter and stink in wild sunlight, gulls
float and scream in the brilliant sky,
polluted waters bob and dazzle, we laugh, our arms ache,
we work together
shoving and kicking and scraping to empty our truckload
over the bank
even though we know
the irony of adding to the Bay fill, the System has us there—
but we love each other and return to the Park.

Thursday, May 15th
At 6 a.m. the ominous zooming, war-sound, of helicopters
breaks into our sleep.

106

To the Park:
ringed with police.
Bulldozers have moved in.
Barely awake, the people—
those who had made for each other
a green place—
begin to gather at the corners.

Their tears fall on sidewalk cement.
The fence goes up, twice a man's height.
Everyone knows (yet no one yet
believes it) what all shall know
this day, and the days that follow:
now, the clubs, the gas,
bayonets, bullets. The War
comes home to us . . .

. . . .

WHAT PEOPLE CAN DO

1. Be in the streets—they're ours!
2. Report any action you have witnessed or been
   involved in that should be broadcast to keep
   the people informed. Especially call to report
   the location of any large groups of people, so
   those people who have been separated may
   regroup . . .
3. The Free Church and Oxford Hall medical
   aid stations need medical supplies, especially:
   —gauze pads
   —adhesive tape
   —plastic squeeze bottles.
4. PLEASE do not go to the Free Church unless
   you have need to.

107

5. Photographers and filmmakers: Contact Park Media Committee.
6. Bail money will be collected at tables outside the COOP grocery stores:
   —Telegraph Ave. store: Monday
   —University Ave. store: Tuesday
   —Shattuck Ave. store: Wed. & Thurs.
7. BRING YOUR KITE AND FLY IT. Use nylon strings. Fly it when you are with a crowd. A helicopter cannot fly too near flying kites.
8. Be your brothers' and sisters' keeper.
9. Take care.

'change is now
change is now
things that seem to be solid are not'

The words came through, transistor
turned up loud. The music, the beat,
lost now, but
the words hang on.

Revolution: a crown of tree
              raises itself out of the heavy
              flood.
                      A branch lifts
                      under null skies' weight
              pushes against
              walls of air, flashing
              clefts in it.

The floodwaters
stir, mud
swirls to the surface.

             A hand, arm,
             lifts in the crawl—
             hands, arms, intricate
                       upflashing—
                                    a sea full of swimmers!
                       their faces' quick steady
                       lift for air—
Maybe what seems
evanescent is solid.

Islands
step out of the waves on rock feet.

(June, 1968—April, 1969)

*For G. who could not help it, I. who saw me,
R. who read me, and M. for everything.*

"The treasure . . . lies buried. There is no need
to seek it in a distant country . . . It is behind
the stove, the center of the life and warmth
that rule our existence, if only we knew how to
unearth it. And yet—there is this strange and
persistent fact, that it is only after . . . a jour-
ney in a distant region, in a new land, that . . .
the inner voice . . . can make itself understood
by us. And to this strange and persistent fact is
added another: that he who reveals to us the
meaning of our . . . inward pilgrimage must be
himself a stranger . . ."

—Heinrich Zimmer

A

Joy—a beginning.   Anguish, ardor.
To relearn the ah! of knowing in unthinking
joy: the belovéd stranger lives.
Sweep up anguish as with a wing-tip,
brushing the ashes back to the fire's core.

B

To be. To love an other only for being.

C

Clear, cool? Not those evasions. The seeing
that burns through, comes through to
the fire's core.

D

In the beginning was delight. A depth
stirred as one stirs fire unthinking.
Dark   dark   dark   . And the blaze illumines
dream.

E

Endless
returning, endless
revolution of dream to ember, ember to anguish,
anguish to flame, flame to delight,
delight to dark and dream, dream to ember

F

that the mind's fire may not fail.
The *vowels of affliction,* of unhealed
not to feel it, uttered,
transformed in utterance
to song.
             Not farewell, not farewell, but faring

111

G

forth into the grace of transformed
continuance, the green meadows
of Grief-Dale where joy grew, flowering
close to the ground, old tales recount,

H

and may be had yet for the harvesting.

        •

I, J

Into the world of continuance, to find
I-who-I-am again, who wanted
to enter a life not mine,
        to leap a wide, deep, swift river.

At the edge, I stand yet. No, I am moving away,
walking away from the unbridged rush of waters towards
'Imagination's holy forest,' meaning to thread its ways,
                that are dark,
and come to my own clearing, where 'dreamy, gloomy,
friendly trees' grow, one by one—but
        I'm not looking where I'm going,
        my head's turned back, to see
           whom I called 'jester': someone dreamed
           on the far bank: not dreamed, seen
in epiphany, as Picasso's bronze *Head of a Jester*
was seen.
        I go stumbling
            (head turned)
                    back to my origins:
(if that's where I'm going)
           to joy, my Jerusalem.

Weeping, gesturing,
I'm a small figure in mind's eye,
diminishing in the sweep of rain or gray tears
that cloud the far shore as jealous rage
clouds love and changes it, changes vision.

.

K

Caritas is what I must travel to.
Through to the fire's core,
an alchemy:
　　　　　caritas, claritas.
But find my face clenched
when I wake at night
　　　　　　　in limbo.

L

Back there forgetting, among the
letters　　folded and put away.
Not uttered.
　　　　'The feel of
not to feel it
was never said . . .' Keats said.
'Desolation . . . Absence an absolute
presence
　　　　calling forth . . .' the jester said
from the far shore ('gravely, ringing his bells,
a tune of sorrow.' I dance to it?)
'You are offhand. The trouble
is concealed?' Isak said,
calling me forth.

.

I am called forth
from time to time.

I was in the time
of desolation.
What light is it
waking me?
            Absence has not become
a presence.
            Lost in the alphabet
            I was looking for
            the word I can't now say
(love)
        and am called forth
        unto the twelfth letter
        by the love in a question.

                    .

M

Honest man, I wanted
                the moon and went
                out to sea to touch
                the moon and

                down a lane of bright
                broken vanishing
                curled pyramids of
                moonwater
                moving
                towards the moon
            and touched
            the luminous dissolving
            half moon
            cold

I am
come back,
humbled, to warm myself,
honest man,

our bed is
            upon the earth
your soul is
            in your body
your mouth
            has found
my mouth once more
—I'm home.

N

Something in me that wants to cling
to *never,*
            wants to have been
            wounded deeper
            burned by the cold moon to cinder,

shrinks as the disk
dwindles to vision
                        numb not to continuance
                        but to that source
                        of mind's fire

                        waning now,
                        no doubt to wax again—

                        yet I perhaps not be there
                        in its light.

O

Hostile.   Ordinary.   Home.
Order.   Alone.   Other.

115

Hostile longing.   Ordinary rose, omnivorous.
              Home, solitude.

Somnolence grotto.
Caught. Lost. Orient almost,
volition.
Own.   Only.

Pain recedes, rising from heart to head
and out.

              Apple thunder, rolling over the
attic floor.

              Yet I would swear
              there had been savage light
              moments before.

P, Q

In childhood dream-play I was always
the knight or squire, not
the lady:
quester, petitioner, win or lose, not
she who was sought.
The initial of quest or question
branded itself long since on the flank
of my Pegasus.
Yet he flies always
home to the present.

R

Released through bars of sorrow
as if not a gate had opened but I
grown intangible had passed through, shadowy,
from dark of yearning into
a soft day, western March;

a thrust of birdsong
parts the gold flowers thickbranching
that roof the path over.

Arms enfold me
tenderly. I am trusted, I trust
the real that transforms me.
                 And relinquish
                 in grief
the seeing that burns through, comes through
to fire's core: transformation, continuance,
              as acts of magic I would perform, are no longer
              articles of faith.

                •

S

Or no: it
slowly becomes known to me:
articles of faith are indeed
rules of the will—graceless,
             faithless.
The door I flung my weight against
was constructed to open   out
              towards me.
In-seeing
to candleflame's
blue ice-cavern, measureless,

may not be forced by sharp
desire.
      The Prince
      turns in the wood: 'Retrace
             thy steps, seek out
     the hut you passed, impatient,
     the day you lost your quarry.

There dwells
a secret. Restore to it
its life.
You will not recognize
your desire until
thou hast it fast, it goeth
aside, it hath
the cunning of quicksilver.'

.

I turn in the forest.
About me the tree-multitudes
twist their roots in earth
to rip it, draw
hidden rivers up into
branch-towers.
Their crowns in the light sway
green beyond vision.
                                All utterance
takes me step by hesitant step towards

T

—yes, to continuance: into
                                that life beyond the dead-end where
(in a desert time of
dry strange heat, of dust
that tinged mountain clouds with copper,
turn of the year impending unnoticed,
the cactus shadows brittle thornstars,
time of
desolation)   I was lost.

.

The forest is holy.
The sacred paths are of stone.
A clearing.
The altars are shifting deposits of pineneedles,
    hidden waters,
    streets of choirwood,
not what the will
thinks to construct for its testimonies.

U

Relearn the alphabet,
relearn the world, the world
understood anew only in doing, understood only as
looked-up-into out of earth,
the heart an eye looking,
the heart a root
planted in earth.
Transmutation is not
under the will's rule.

V

Vision sets out
journeying somewhere,
walking the dreamwaters:
arrives
not on the far shore but upriver,
a place not evoked, discovered.

       ·

W

Heart breaks but mends
like good bone.

It's the vain will
wants to have been wounded deeper,
burned by the cold moon to cinder.

Wisdom's a stone
dwells in forgotten pockets—
lost, refound, exiled—
revealed again
in the palm of
mind's hand, moonstone
of wax and wane, stone pulse.

Y

Vision will not be used.
Yearning will not be used.
Wisdom will not be used.
Only the vain will
strives to use and be used,
comes not to fire's core
but cinder.

Z

Sweep up
anguish as with a wing-tip:

the blaze addresses
a different darkness:
absence has not become
the transformed presence the will
looked for,
but other: the present,

that which was poised already in the ah! of praise.

Silent, about-to-be-parted-from house.
Wood creaking, trying to sigh, impatient.
Clicking of squirrel-teeth in the attic.
Denuded beds, couches stripped of serapes.

Deep snow shall block all entrances
and oppress the roof and darken
the windows.   O Lares,
don't leave.
The house yawns like a bear.
Guard its profound dreams for us,
that it return to us when we return.